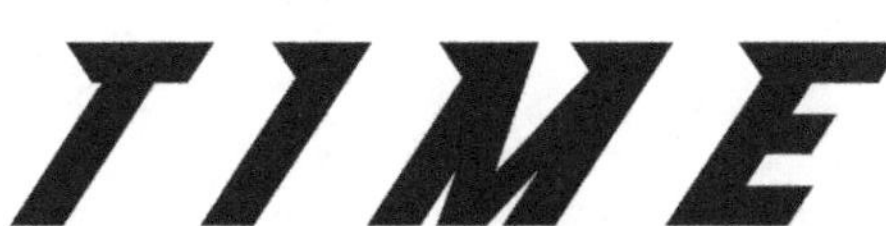

TIME ON THE MOVE

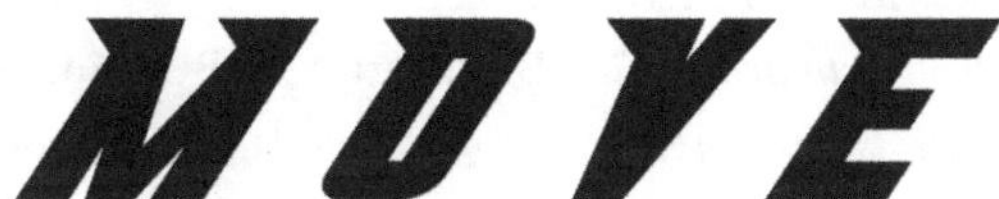

BARRY WALLENSTEIN
PHOTOS: BARBARA ROSENTHAL

XANADU PRESS

Praise for his Previous Works

Wallenstein, who frequently performs his work to jazz accompaniment, has mastered a poetic voice with the hypnotic, insinuating tones of a tenor sax.e summons a cool music from the world's mayhem. — *Philip Fried*

These poems "swell with silver and fill with gold" and have just the right tinge of irony, warmed by a snifter of fine cognac...quietly but unflinchingly confronting "the thought that blocks the rhythm" — *Mikhail Horowitz*

Syntactically quirky, varied, these poems speak eloquently to his jazz artist's concern - with love, death, sex and satire. — *Colette Inez*

His poems—hip, sexy, knowing—bring to the page the voice of a poet who has seen it all but never loses his capacity to be surprised and delighted by this phantasmagoria we call the world. — *Richard Tillinghast*

There is an off-handed canniness of phrasing about these poems, a way of registering emotional freight and the time it takes to carry it ... a tribute ... to his lifelong love of jazz, and the source of both jazz and poetry, the syncopated heart. — *William Matthews*

...magic, seductive, cryptic, more than a little frightening. — *Alicia Ostriker*

[Wallenstein's] work is a substance milled or ground from the wall stone of this realist of all possible worlds. The urban muddle of street and inspiration, of will and desire is all lashed together as material life. ... nevertheless, it is a music ... to hear it is strength enough... this is the real work. — *Amiri Baraka*

Barry Wallenstein is a splendid urban poet whose ear is alert to the music of New York dialects, generational inflections, jazz. — *Marilyn Hacker*

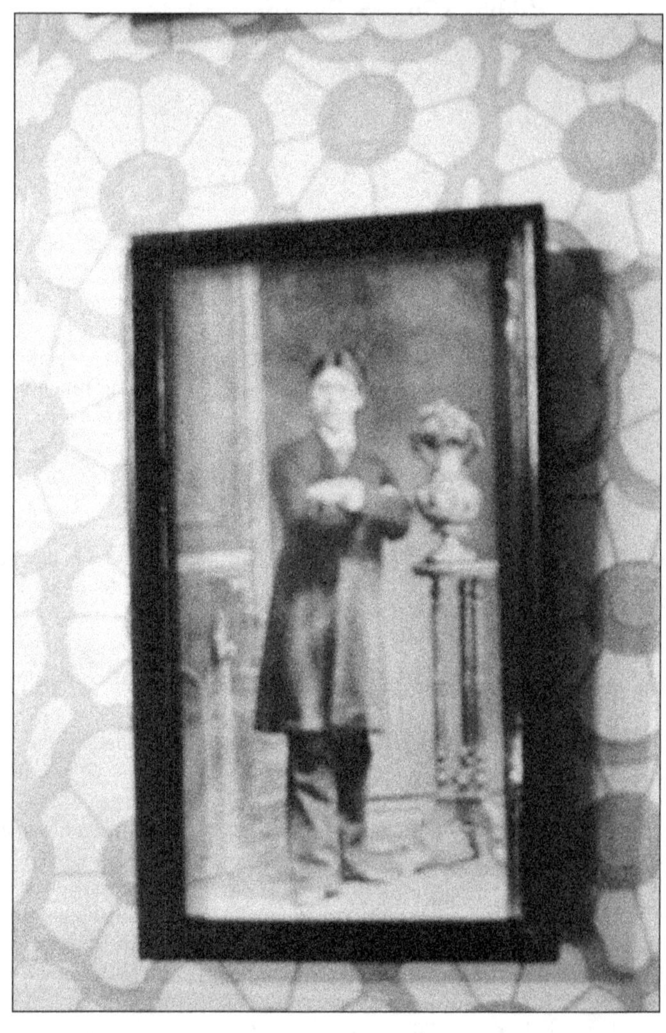

"Time on the Move" © copyright 2020 *Barry Wallenstein*

TIME

ON THE

MOVE

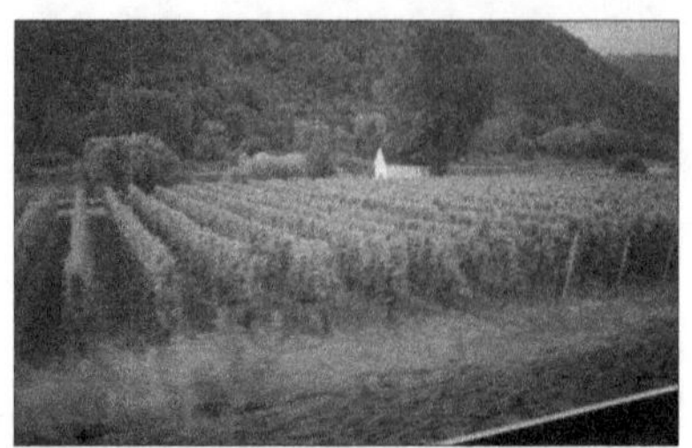

TABLE OF CONTENTS, TEXTS

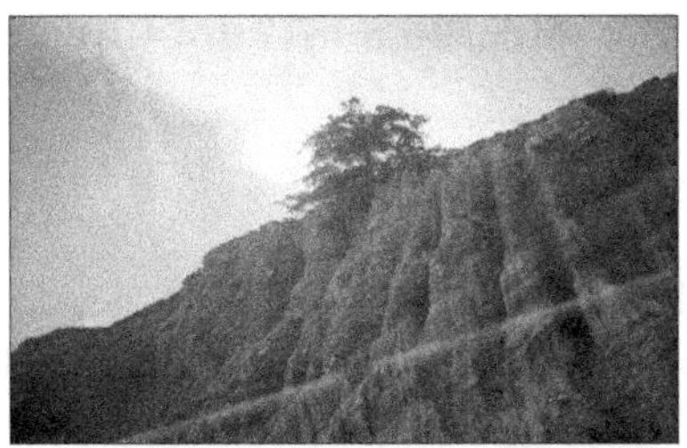

Table of Contents, Photographs

Author's Introduction

I began reading poetry for delight when in elementary school and started writing verse in high school. It was at NYU when I fell under the influence of the poet/critic M. L. Rosenthal and became devoted to poetry. My first book of poems, with a forward by Mack Rosenthal, was published by BOA Editions in 1977 and many of the poems there were written in my 20s. The theme of time, kissing cousin of mortality, was already present. Here is one very early example:

The Falling Apart of Time

My brain is beside me
or on the glass table
looking or itself looking like
a dropped watch.

Everywhere, I mean near me,
the parts
or loose connections fall about.
A wheel is moving or rolling
into an object which collapses.

That too takes time.

My grandfather's watch
was gold.
It ran through him through all the states
into a long pocket,
his gentleman's trousers.

In more recent times,
I do the watch trick:
my smallest hand, the second hand,
falls off;
my crystal, all in fragments,
catches light & cuts.
And my movements,
all my fine movements,
my jewels and bearings,
wind down and spring shut.

More recently, as I approach the great age of 80, time has become, if not an obsession, a preoccupation. The poems in this chapbook are on this theme and its fleeting certainty.

One of the poems from my last poetry book, At the Surprise Hotel addresses this theme
more or less directly:

Tomorrow

When that lovely word comes true,
the shadow that fooled no one lifts,
and we celebrate:
the gold comes teaming –
the morning stretch,
the fresh mouth after the brush
for many – the first coffee or tea.
And then adventure begins
and proves the idea of tomorrow
grander even than luck or love
or holidays with no end of money.

Without tomorrow –as idea or fact:
no hook to hang anything,
no pot to piss in,
no pot no gin,
no kiss from mother, father, wife, or kids,
the old friend who drops by,
the new friend to embrace
and discover her story;
no taste on the tongue
no bitter aftertaste to spit
no failed memory – but to become one.

Banish the thought that blocks the rhythm;
advancing age supports the pretense of wisdom.

Almost all my writing life I've enjoyed performing and recording my poetry in the
company of jazz musicians. When I recite the poem above, the music stops before I speak
the final couplet.

—Barry Wallenstein

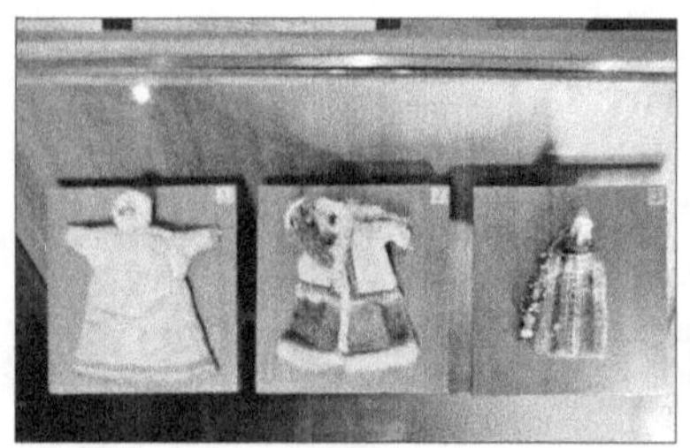
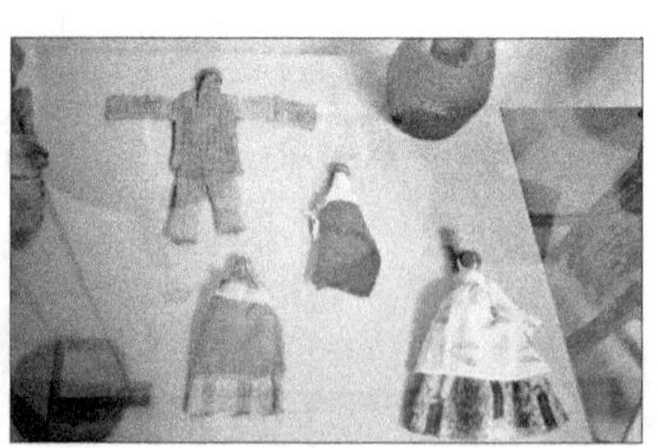
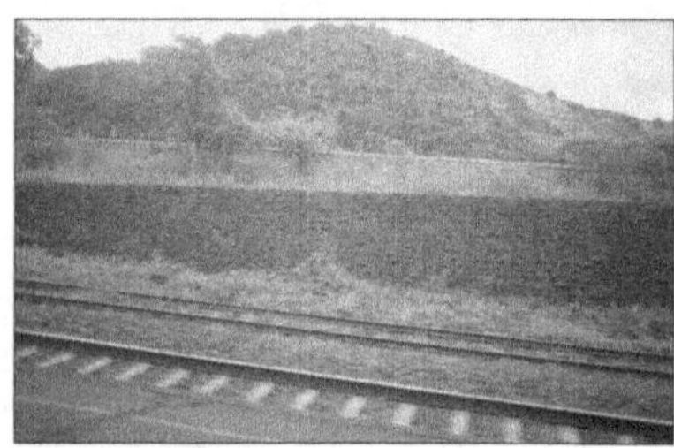
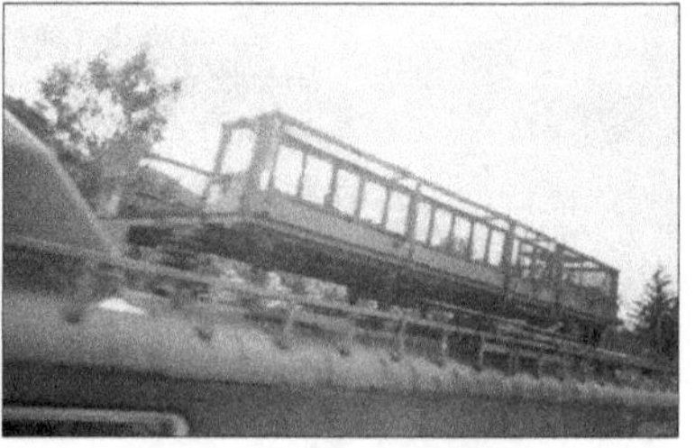

TIME

Under every field of snow
lies a rising field of clover.

Remember we never wasted a moment—
not a jot lost in the rush –
your back room, an hourglass on its side.

"Yesterday I was five"
the six-year-old insists,
and at twenty the young man knows
that "yesterday I was five"
was true that day
and will always be.

The abandoned train rails rust
in the changing seasons' claws.
Still, do not play dead
on those antique tracks
as they bend around the hills,
flattening capsules of time,

and watch for speeding trains
along the glistening bars.

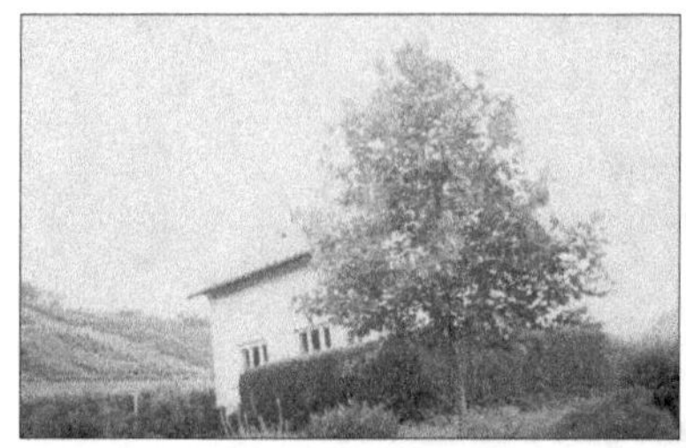 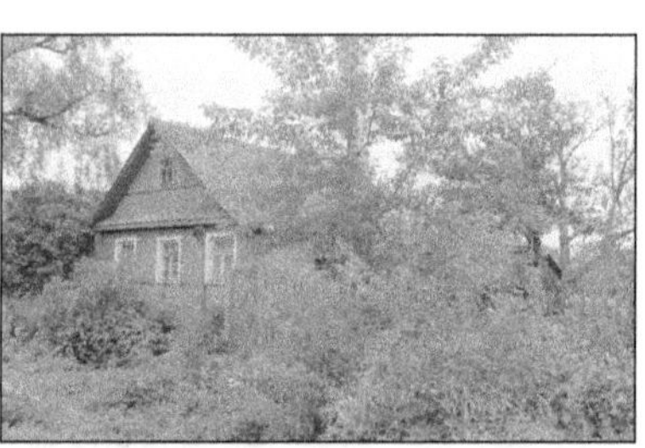

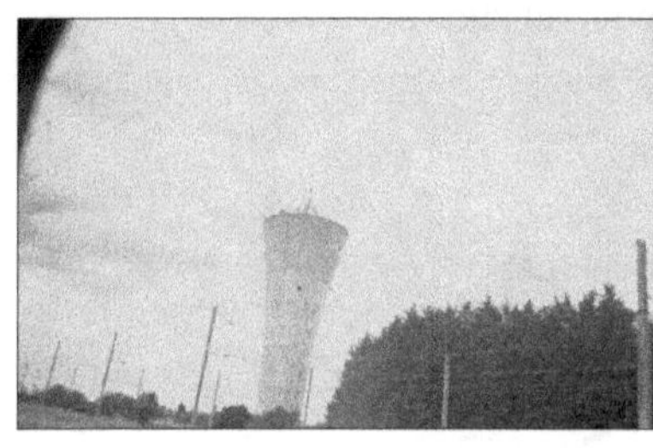 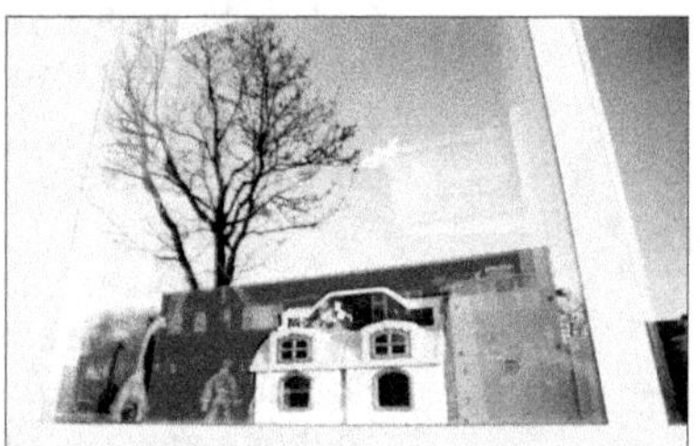

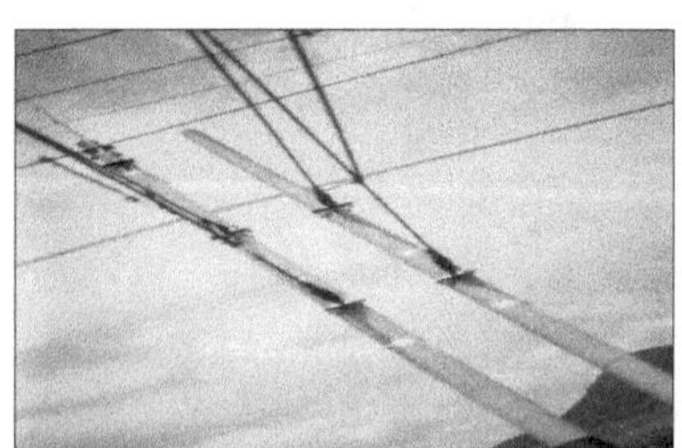 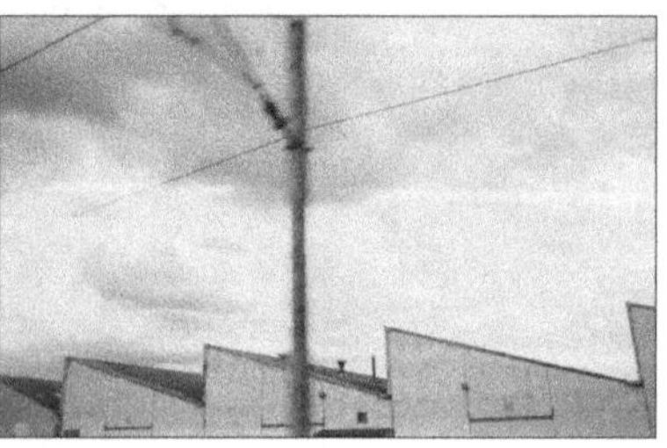

Autumn Leaf

From my image on the pond,
I know my blush is deep,
my edges curl,
and my stem, though attached,
is drying. I'll be on you soon.

Tonight's predicted rainstorm
may sail me to your surface.
Once that happens,
that inescapable small tumble,
we'll be a spectacle of color.

But I'll hang here a little longer.
It may not rain after all,
so, there's extra time.
While you wait for me,
I'll hold fast to the old apple tree.

Come spring
I could be lingering still,
a last leaf upon the tree.

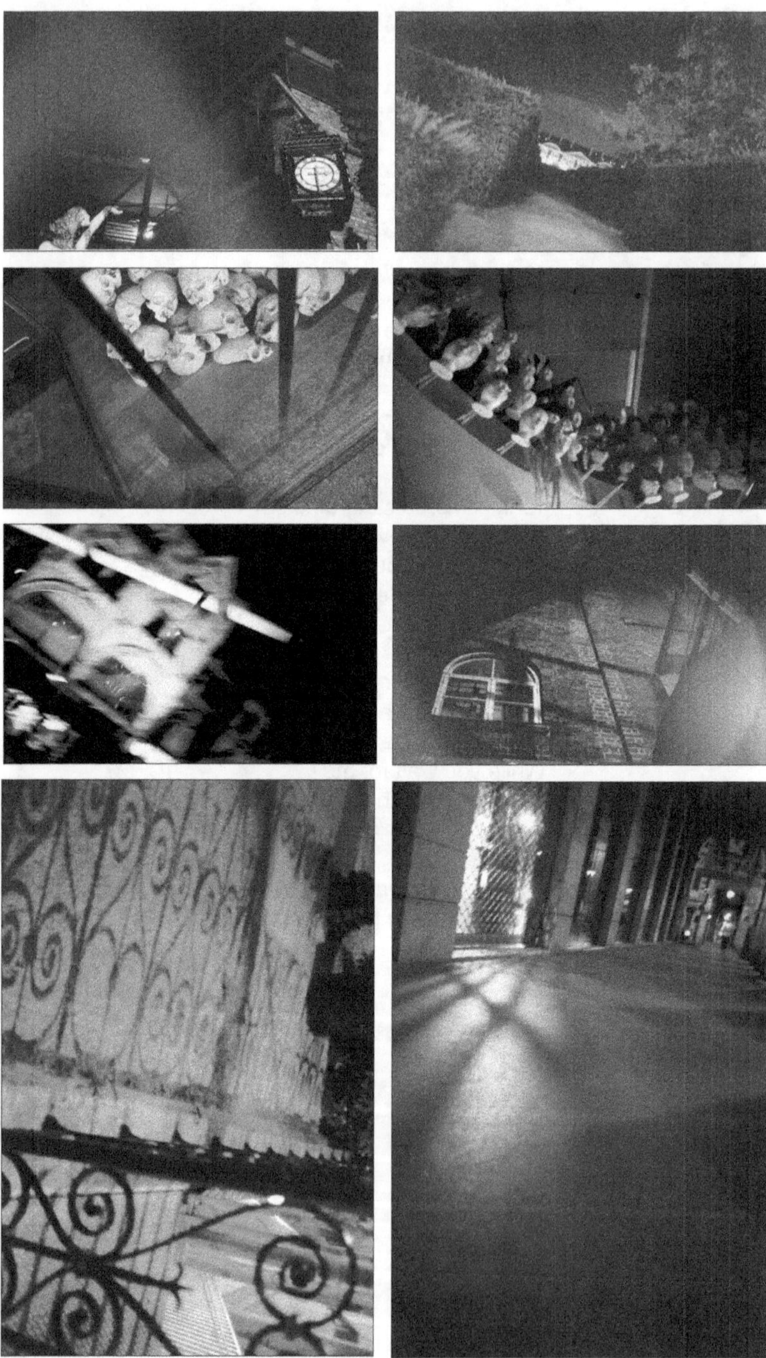

STILL HERE

I stumble upon each o'clock
crack my head upon a rock,
and I'm lifted away — a cloud on a breeze.

A monster reaches out of the bog,
its hairy hands, and nostrils flaring;
its reach is not related to love,
so, I blink back the danger
and look into my hand—amazing construction.

This pain – spinal awareness –
tightening rings – engenders rest –
always at the chimes of afternoon.
Dreams come tumbling
into my daytime bedtime rest.

Children in the house around the clock,
my luck enough to repel the rock
or staunch the blood should it flow—
they're gone where they go.

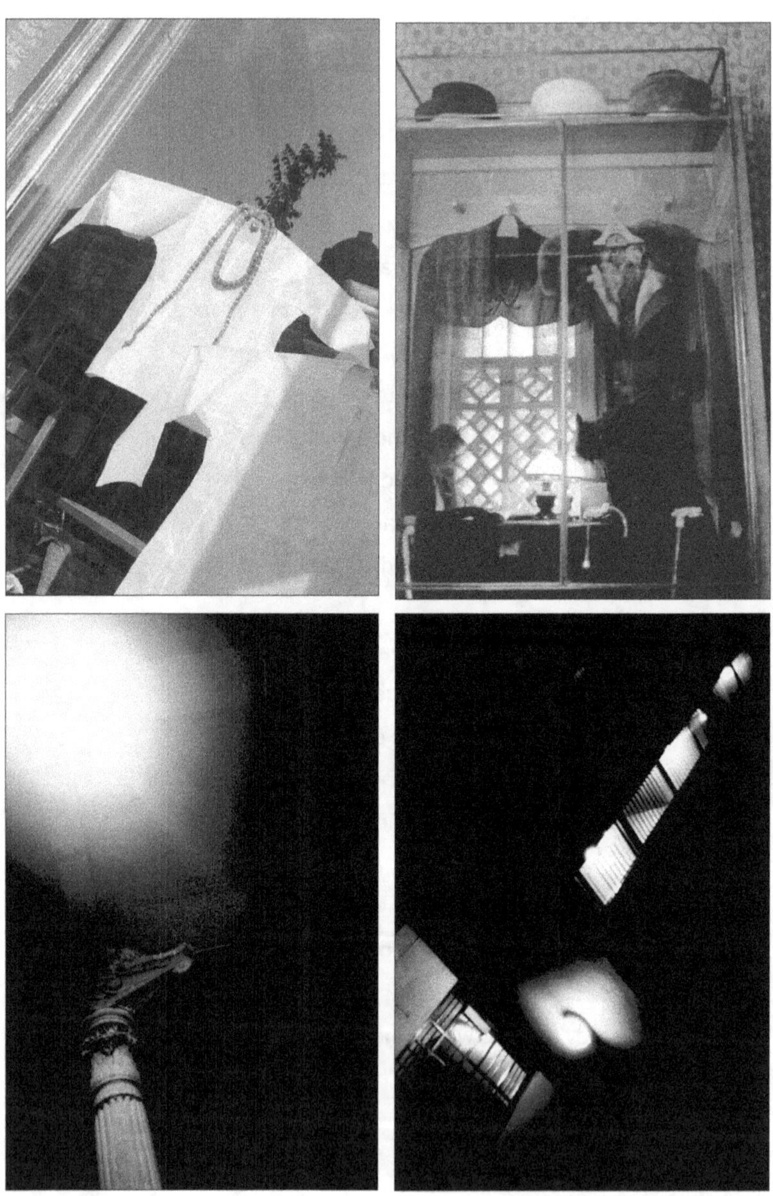

Eventually

the friendship will clarify or die,
the wound heal or fester,
the loose tooth tighten or fall out,
the falsehood reveal itself
and the fabricator be put in chains.

Eventually, the traffic will untie
and the bumpers locked together
will separate, and the cars will hum
along the freeway,
free in their release
all the way to Tuscaloosa.

Eventually, the seas will rise higher,
the stars come closer,
and a new species,
as full of accident as our own,
will rise up to build and knock down things
for a very long minute.

Eventually,
we'll ship out dressed like quality
to have a magic time in the coming months,
and our world, impressed by the wake of our passage,
will whisper within itself,
"maybe tonight."

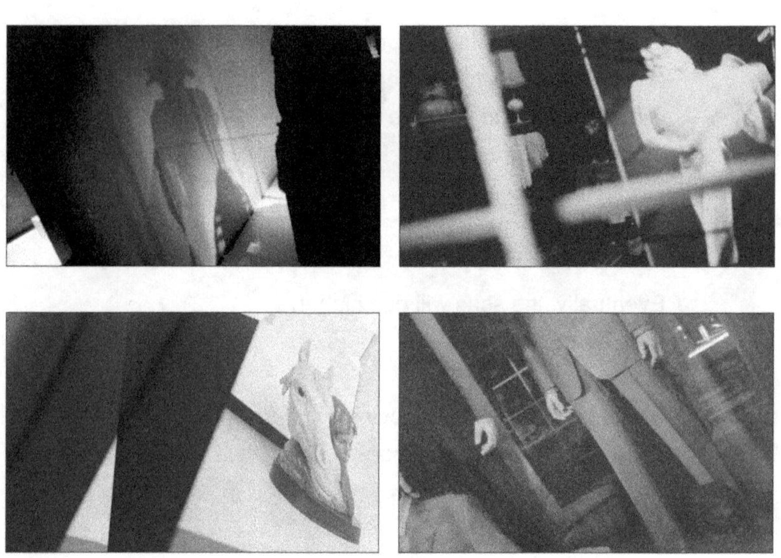

THUS FAR

So far, we've not been together
long enough
for the distant bell's ringing
to thin in the wind
or become tangled filament
in memory's wild hair.

So far, it takes a year or more
for the sheep to fatten,
meat to be sliced,
placed on the plate, eaten,
and the gravy savored.

As our meal baked,
we talked, basted and added spices.
The wait felt less heavy
than lint on a blind man's coat.
The wrinkles and portents
slept in the shadows, were minuscule.

So far neither of us have thighs
that are shudder-proof
or wise to the number of days
allowed in the arc of
what we've built
in this year of our allowance.

Thus far, our lamps' red wicks
burn on two flames;
slowly they go down
leaving the scent of paraffin
as the sparks flicker
and still manage to glow.

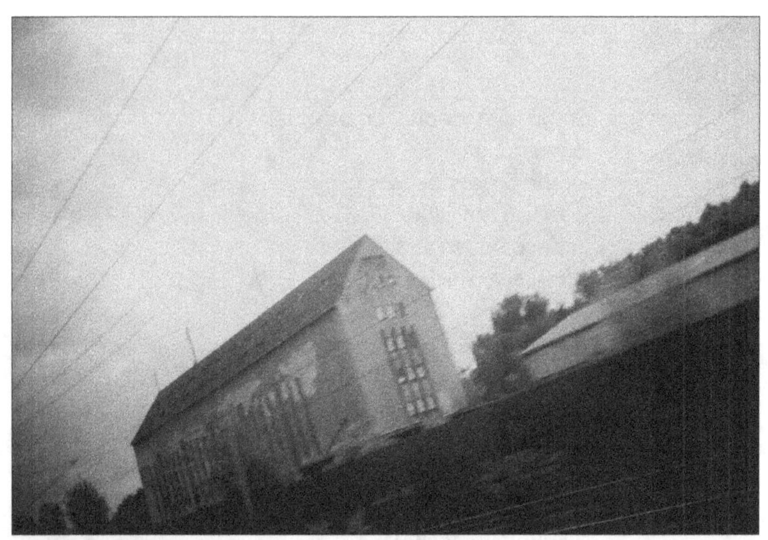

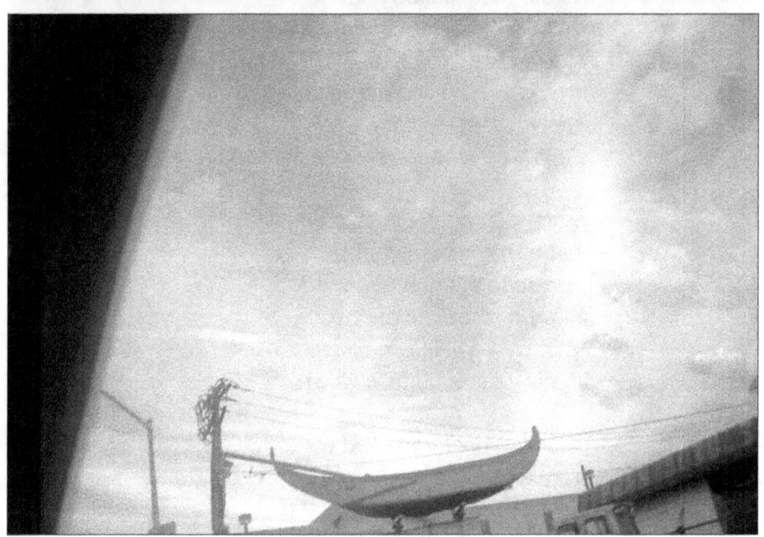

WASTING TIME

The sign above the train station

reads *Don't Waste Time*.
The soon-to-be-passengers,
blank faces bent over watches
and smart phones, don't see the sign,
nor do they regard their company
god-given.

But one citizen – an old guy –
does see the sign and kicks back:
"No, time wastes you / I mean us
including me – far enough along time's wire
to be about wasted,
and all those mushrooms
expanding the moments in my time
were not lost; I was busy in the trip

and after." If only we *could* waste time
or any of us alone or together
diminish the idea, cripple it.
Other beasts wile away the hours;
the lion freed from his cage –
feels fantastic in the air –
out of time entirely,
he becomes his species.

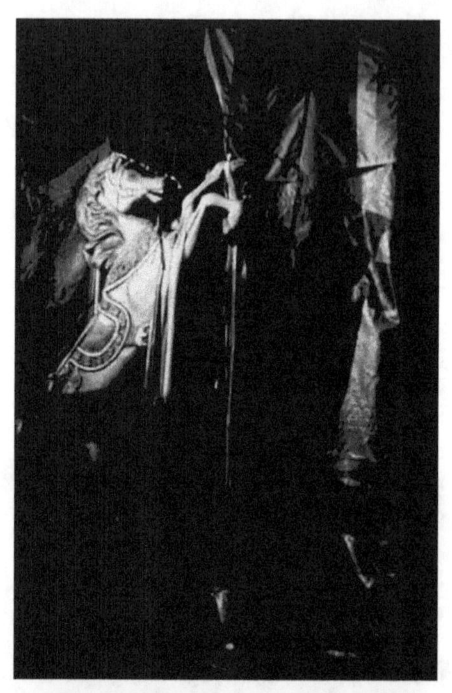

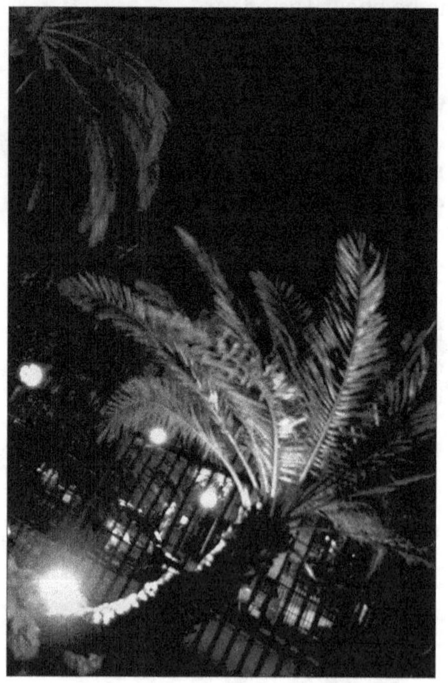

YESTERDAY, TODAY AND TOMORROW

Yesterday he was buoyant,
and he didn't need the sea
to float him above all cares;
he stayed cheery
all of that day,

and when he collided with an object,
it was painless; nothing ever broke.
The arms and hands he ran into
were embracing
and lasted deep into evening.

Then morning arrived
on an aerial steed
flying joyously
into the new day
but unease had come along
for the ride.

He slipped slowly into his nest of worries.
A clock-watcher obsessed,
he lamented the day for its dearth of hours.
Then, here it is again, time to go to bed again
and envision another tomorrow
as if it were promised.

ABOUT THE AUTHOR

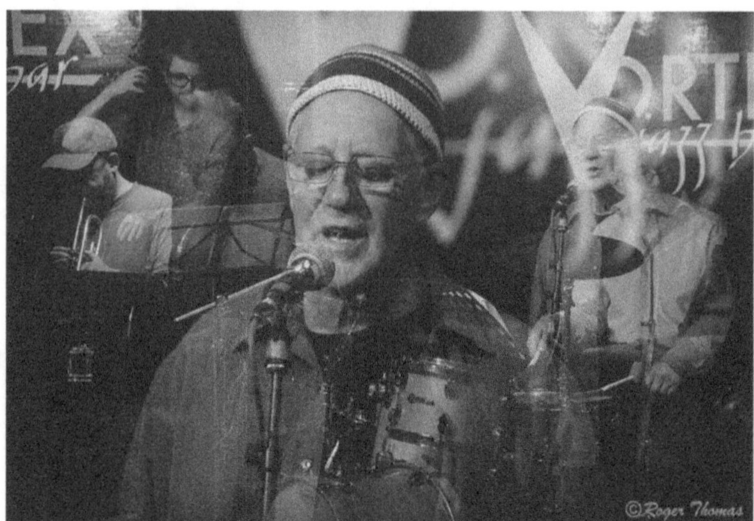

Barry Wallenstein is the author of eight collections of poetry, the most recent being *At the Surprise Hotel and Other Poems* [Ridgeway Press, 2016] and *Drastic Dislocations: New and Selected Poems* [New York Quarterly Books, 2012]. His poetry has appeared in over 100 journals, including *Ploughshares*, *The Nation*, and *American Poetry Review*. A special interest is his presentation of poetry readings in collaboration with jazz. He has made nine recordings of his poetry with jazz, the most recent being *Lisbon Sunset* (2018), *What Was, Was* (2015) and *Lucky These Days* (2013). Barry is Emeritus Professor of Literature and Creative Writing at the City University of New York and an editor of the journal, *American Book Review*.

www.barrywallenstein.com

Photo © Roger Thomas: Barry Wallenstein performing his poetry to jazz accompaniment at the Vortex Jazz Club, London, September, 2015.

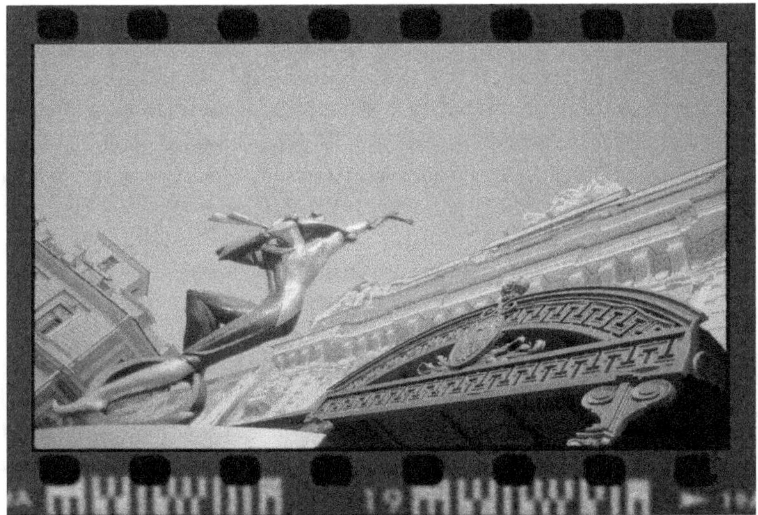

Down the steep, thin wooden stairs of the famed but now closed Cornelia Street Café, in a narrow, red-lit roomful of little tables and a one-foot bar, a space the type we here in Greenwich Village used to call a "cahv," spelled "cave," I first heard the poetry of Barry Wallenstein about two years ago. Light piano, brushy drum and alto sax accompanied his melodic, rhythmic spoken words, each line of which evoked images that ran in my mind not as illustrations, but as parallel tonation. I believed I was listening to surreal narratives, fictions, stories of anxious people and palpable locations.

Upon leaving, I offered him a book trade for my novel with photos between the chapters, and was genuinely surprised to see line breaks in his chapbook! Orally, he produced magical stories and pictures that in text-graphics appeared on the page as brief lines recognizable as poetry. When I read them to myself that night, my mind-ears heard his cadences, but on my mind-screen were some of my own surreal photos. I travel to do shows and readings in many countries, always capturing images on film that seem to have more to do with my own anxieties and imbalances and speeds and sense of fleeting time and ceaseless motion than they do with any of the cities, countries or even continents I'm photographing in. That same kind of parallel non-illustration that my photographs have in relation to their locations, is what I felt they had to Barry Wallenstein's poetry. I use both black and white and color film; these were all shot black and white. They are full frame 35mm, no crop or manipulations. The numbers indicate processing month/year/roll/frame.

My studio, eMediaLoft, had launched a small image-text press the previous year, Xanadu, so with some trepidation, I asked Barry if I might publish a small book of his poems with pages of my photos selected to appear with them, like the music that most often does. With more trust than any other author or artist I have ever worked with, he said yes immediately, knowing only the 58 pictures that appear in the novel he received in trade, not even asking to see my choices for this book now, which he plans to wait for publication to be surprised by at its launch, as if for a festschrift, at the Lower East Side artspace Lichtundfire, on February 13, 2020, his 80th birthday.

barbararosenthal.org   BARBARA ROSENTHAL

ABOUT THE PRESS

XANADU PRESS is the mixed image/text-based of the two imprints published by eMediaLoft.org. It produces books in which pictures and texts are imaginative, and visually linked. The other, WASHINGTON STREET PRESS, produces text-based books of fiction and exposition. Both are designed and edited by media and performance artist and writer Barbara Rosenthal. Her monthly column of philosophy about the interconnection of art and artist, *A Crack in the Sidewalk,* appears in *Ragazine,* and her bookworks are in the collections of The Whitney, MoMA, Tate, Berlin Kunstbibliotek, Artpool Budapest, et al. No submissions are accepted; publication is by invitation only.

eMediaLoft.org is located in the neon-effused live-work loft Rosenthal shares with Director Emeritus, Bill Creston, within the Westbeth Arts Complex on the Hudson River in the Highline / West Village neighborhood of NYC. It is a privately funded loose consortium of living and recently deceased individuals who create(d) hard-to-place, hard-to-categorize works, primarily using replicable or recordable media: camera and electronic arts, performance, audio and writing, with a strong conceptual base and discernible philosophical perspective.

Acknowledgments

"Tomorrow" – from *At the Surprise Hotel*, Ridgeway Press, 2016

"Yesterday, Today & Tomorrow" – *Manhattan Review,* Vol. 19, No. 1, Fall/Winter 2019—2020. pp121 - 123